WHY DO FLIES LIKE GROSS STUFF?

by Ellen Labrecque

Raintree is an imprint of Capstone Global Library Limited, a company incorporated in England and Wales having its registered office at 264 Banbury Road, Oxford, OX2 7DY – Registered company number: 6695582

www.raintree.co.uk
myorders@raintree.co.uk

Edited by Megan Peterson
Designed by Ted Williams
Original illustrations © Capstone Global Library Limited 2022
Picture research by Jo Miller
Production by Spencer Rosio
Originated by Capstone Global Library Ltd
Printed and bound in India

978 1 3982 1563 4 (hardback)
978 1 3982 1571 9 (paperback)

British Library Cataloguing in Publication Data
A full catalogue record for this book is available from the British L

Acknowledgements
We would like to thank the following for permission to reproduce photographs: Capstone Press, 20, (pencil) 21; Dreamstime: Cherdchai Chaivimol, 11, Gaspert, 8, Ianthraves, 13, Jordan Roper, 7; iStockphoto: arlindo71, 6, egiss, 19; Shutterstock: Breaking The Walls, (ink) Cover, design element, Ernie Cooper, (fly) Cover , frank60, 15, Latte Art, 5, Monster e, 14, owatta, (mark) Cover, design element, suesse, bottom right 21, SURAJKMALIPhotography, 17, Vinicius R. Souza, 9

CONTENTS

Here come the flies...4

No nose? No problem! 6

No straw needed 8

Sticky feet...10

Fly babies 12

Bloodthirsty 14

Helpful flies 16

    Draw a fly 20

    Glossary 22

    Find out more 23

    Index..24

Words in **bold** are in the glossary.

Here come the flies

Flies are everywhere. These **insects** buzz around old food. They land in dirty rain puddles. They fly around smelly rubbish. They dig into piles of poo.

Most people avoid these yucky things. Not flies! Why can't flies stay away from gross stuff? Because it's their food!

5

No nose? No problem!

Flies live everywhere on Earth. For every person, there are about 17 million flies. And none of them has a nose! So how do they sniff out all that yucky stuff?

Flies smell with their **antennae**. Two antennae stick out from their heads. Flies use them to smell for food. Flies also have **compound eyes**. They can see in almost all directions at once.

eye

eye

No straw needed

Flies may smell with their antennae. But they taste with their feet! This is why flies land on your food. They want a taste of your meal too.

Flies can't chew. When they land on food, they throw up. Fly vomit turns the food into liquid. Flies slurp up the food with a straw-like mouthpart. Yum? Yuck is more like it.

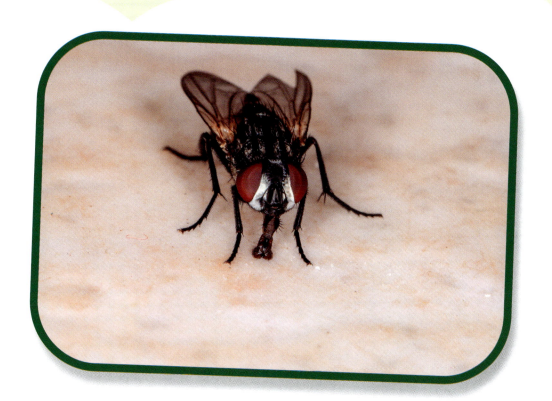

Sticky feet

Flies will walk anywhere for a gross meal. They can even crawl upside down! Tiny hairs cover a fly's feet. Fly feet also release a sticky liquid. This liquid helps flies stick to surfaces.

Dirt, dust and **germs** stick to fly feet. These germs spread to everything flies touch. Germs can make people and animals sick.

Fly babies

Most flies only live about one month. But females can lay more than 1,000 eggs. They lay eggs in warm, wet places. They often choose piles of rotten food and poo.

Fly eggs hatch into **maggots**. They look like tiny worms. Maggots eat the poo and rubbish. It helps them grow. Maggots become adult flies in about two weeks.

13

Bloodthirsty

Ouch! Have you ever been bitten by a mosquito? Mosquitoes are a type of fly. Their bites leave behind itchy, red bumps.

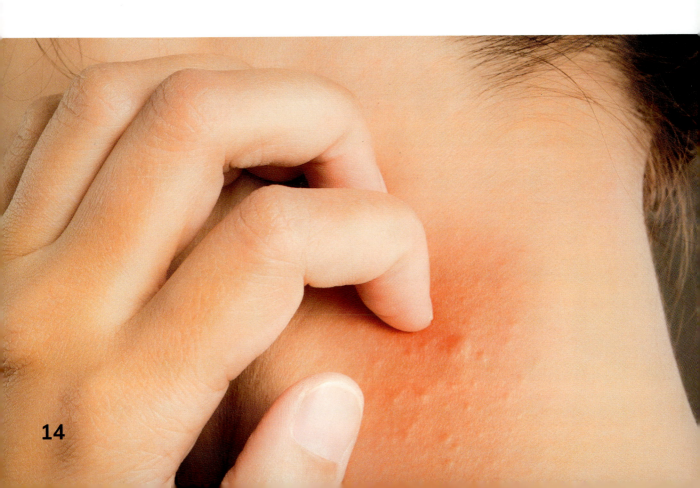

Why do they bite? To feast on our blood! They also drink blood from animals. Only female mosquitoes eat blood. They need blood to grow new eggs.

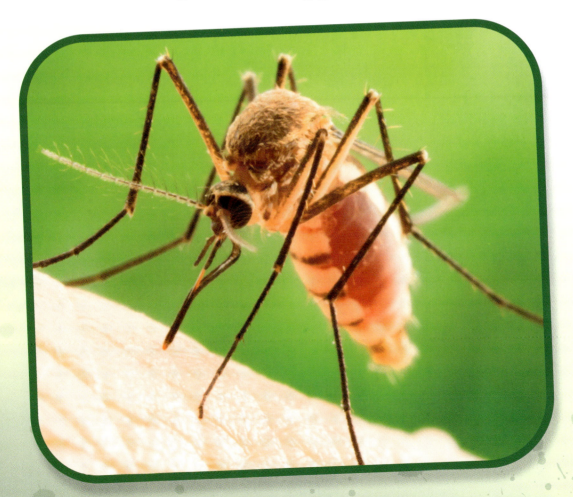

Helpful flies

Flies can be gross. But they are also helpful. Some flies carry **pollen** from plant to plant. This helps plants grow.

Other flies help clean the earth. **Blowflies** lay eggs in dead animals. The maggots eat the animals. Other flies eat dead plants. They help put **nutrients** back into the soil.

Flies have been around for 250 million years. They will probably always like gross stuff. But we need flies to help make food and flowers. We need them for clean-up duty. What you think is yucky, flies think is yummy!

Draw a fly

What you need:

- paper
- pencil
- felt-tip pens or crayons

What to do:

1. Draw a fly. Use the picture below to help you.

2. Label the fly's legs, wings, head, eyes and antennae.

3. Colour the picture of the fly. Flies come in many colours. Use your imagination.

4. Draw gross stuff around the fly. You can draw things like mud or rubbish. Your fly will love that!

21

Glossary

antennae feelers on an insect's head

blowfly large, shiny blue or green fly that lays eggs in poo or on dead animals

compound eye eye made up of lots of lenses; compound eyes are good for seeing fast-moving things

germ tiny living thing that causes sickness

insect small animal with a hard outer shell, six legs, three body sections and two antennae

maggot larva, or early form, of certain flies

nutrient something that is needed by people, animals and plants to stay healthy and strong

pollen powder made by flowers to help them create new seeds

Find out more

Books

The Book of Brilliant Bugs, Jess French
(DK Children, 2020)

Insects (Animal Kingdom), Janet Riehecky
(Raintree, 2017)

Insects and Spiders: Explore Nature with Fun Facts and Activities (Nature Explorers), DK
(DK Children, 2019)

Websites

www.bbc.co.uk/bitesize/topics/z6882hv
Learn more about animals, from mammals to minibeasts.

**www.dkfindout.com/uk/animals-and-nature/
animal-kingdom**
Find out more about the animal kingdom.

Index

antennae 7, 8

blood 15
blowflies 16

compound eyes 7

eggs 12, 15, 16

feet 8, 10
female flies 12, 15
food 4, 7, 9, 12, 18

germs 10

maggots 12, 16
mosquitoes 14, 15
mouthparts 9

plants 16
pollen 16
poo 4, 12

rubbish 4, 12

smelling 7, 8

tasting 8